The Archbishop's
School of Life after Death

Written by David W

❦ ❦ ❦

GW00976340

Too Good to be True?

As a clergyman who has worked for the last thirteen years in rural England, I've become familiar with an odd contradiction in people's attitude towards death. In general – say, when the subject gets raised in the pub or at a supper party – people tend to say things like, 'Well, when you go, you go', or (especially the men): 'It's out like a light, and that's that.' In other words, when they stop to think about an event that will happen to every single one of us sooner or later, they regard it as the end – the terminus of the journey of life.

On the other hand, when I visit people who have been bereaved, or to prepare a funeral, or talk to them months later, I find a quite different attitude. It's true that some do speak of the one they loved as having 'gone', but they also speak of them as though they still existed. 'Yes, Dad would like that hymn,' they say. They'll often go further. 'She won't be happy unless there's a garden up there!' 'He'll be so pleased Bolton have got promoted.' Now people are speaking of the dead as real, living persons, even though located somewhere else – rather as though they'd emigrated to Australia in the days before phones and air travel.

The two attitudes reflect a strange conflict in our thinking. Rationally, most of us can't see how there can be life beyond death. After all, when things die – the hamster, the rhododendron bush, that troublesome wasp – they stay dead. We know what 'dead' means. Bitter as it is to swallow, the evidence of our eyes and of our experience of life tells us that death is the end.

Death – End or Beginning?

On the other hand, there seems to be some deep-rooted, instinctive 'feeling' that – where human beings are concerned, at least – death is not the end: not the end of life, not the end of love, not the end of the journey. That is why any discussion of life beyond death is much more than an academic exercise. Perfectly sane and normal people sit by the grave and talk to their loved one. They light a candle for them in church on All Saints' Day, and remember them in their prayers. And behind it all they cherish a hope, faint at times, but persistent, that somewhere, somehow, they will see them again.

Some would dismiss this as simply a matter of 'the wish being father to the thought' – 'Yes, it's a nice idea, but frankly it's too good to be true.' For others – the majority, I suspect – it's a kind of incoherent longing. While we can't visualise

heaven, and may have only the haziest concept of God, something tells us that there is a truth here that is deeper than mere optimism. For instance, in conversations with other people who, like myself, have lost a very close partner or a cherished child, I have never met one who answered the question 'Do you believe they no longer exist?' in the affirmative. Most are emphatic that the one they love still exists, even though they can't imagine how or where.

Of course, among them are some who are convinced Christians, with an absolute conviction about what Jesus called 'eternal life'. They have in their minds a much clearer understanding of a divine purpose which does not end with the death of a human body. It may seem to others like a brave whistling in the dark, but they know that it is built on surer foundations than that. It is those foundations which this booklet sets out to explore.

Section 1 *What's the evidence?*

On the surface, the short answer is 'not much'. We all know what 'dead' looks like, whether it be dead leaves, dead plants, dead pets or – sadly – dead people. The case against life beyond death is simply put: look around you, decide from experience. 'There is a time to be born, and a time to die': isn't that in the Bible? (Yes, it is, in Ecclesiastes 3:2.)

Yet there is more, much more, to the argument than that. If it were simply a question of looking around us and learning from experience, why would so many highly intelligent people, in every culture and throughout the whole of human history, have believed otherwise? Surely they are not all guilty of naive, wishful thinking?

I for one don't believe they are. I believe there is 'evidence' which, taken with our human 'hunch' that there's 'more to life than this one', adds up to a convincing case.

Some of the 'evidence' for life beyond death comes from what we might call 'paranormal experiences'. Occasionally, it is well documented and convincing. Of course, Christians don't think of the life beyond as inhabited by discarnate ghosts and spirits; but it's hard to deny that some people, in some situations, have experienced contact with those who have died, sometimes through what we might choose to call 'spirits'.

There is one extremely well-documented case from the last century, the so-called 'Chaffin Will' case. It is told in full detail by Rosalind Heywood in her book *Man's Concern with Death*. It concerns James Chaffin, a farmer in North

Carolina, who died in 1921. Fourteen years later his younger son, James, began to have vivid dreams of his father appearing in an old overcoat that he remembered him wearing, and saying that there was a will hidden in its pocket. He found the coat at his older brother's house and also found a note in the pocket, directing him to chapter 27 of the book of Genesis in the old family Bible. In the presence of witnesses the Bible was found, and sure enough there was a more recent will than the one they already had – a will which was accepted as valid by State law.

There are, of course, many such stories in print, though few which are as difficult to refute. As Rosalind Heywood remarks, 'Whatever the explanation, there is *something* to be explained.' There certainly is, though these, and similar, instances can only be used as evidence of a continuity of human self-consciousness after death in some circumstances.

★ ★ ★ ★

It is important to stress that such 'evidence' is not at all to be taken as proof of the truth of what we know as 'spiritualism' (that is, communicating with the dead through spirits, mediums and séances) which is explicitly forbidden in the Bible (Leviticus 20:27). Neither is it by any means evidence for belief in reincarnation, which involves the rebirth of individual 'souls' in different forms, whether human, animal or even plant. Again, the Bible is quite clear that we live once, we die once and there is one 'judgement' after death (see Hebrews 9:27).

Near-Death Experiences

So-called 'near-death' experiences provide rather more convincing evidence that death is a far more complex matter than simply the switching off of a human life. They have been well documented in medical circles in recent years, and have some recurrent elements to them that seem to throw light on the whole process of death and dying.

A 'near-death' experience occurs when a patient, usually in hospital, either very nearly dies or is, for a short while, clinically 'dead' but recovers. In many well-recorded instances the person involved has had a similar experience of travelling along a corridor of bright light towards a welcoming figure. They have not found this experience at all frightening; rather the contrary, they have been deeply reassured by it. Some have professed themselves sorry to have been brought back to 'life'! Some of these experiences are documented in a book by two Americans, Otis and Haraldson (*At the Hour of Death*, 1977), based on evidence from over 1,700 doctors who had encountered similar responses in interviews with patients. Of course, such phenomena are not 'proof' of life after death, but taken together they do at least help to undermine the glib assertion that 'there's no evidence for it'.

Back From the Grave

However, the Christian case does not rest on paranormal experiences of this kind, even though they do serve to undermine the simplistic argument that 'there's no evidence' for life beyond death. As someone once said to me, 'What we want is someone who's been dead to come back and tell us what it's like.' I agreed, but said that we had precisely that, in the person of Jesus.

> "*It is not so much that we have to go to heaven. We have to do this too. But heaven has to come to us first. Heaven has to begin in ourselves.*"
>
> (Paterson Smyth)

Jesus certainly died on a cross, probably in 30 AD under the proconsul Pontius Pilate. Equally certainly, his followers became convinced that he had risen from the dead and that they had seen and talked with him. They were so sure of this that many of them were prepared to die for this belief. The resurrection of Jesus is really the linchpin of the Christian belief in life beyond death. If it actually happened, then in one case, at least, there is life after death. Not only that, but it makes Jesus a primary witness to what such life is like.

From the resurrection of Jesus we can deduce two things. The first is that life after death is possible. The second is that what he had to say about it is more convincing than any number of ingenious theories on the subject.

Few people nowadays, and none at all who are taken seriously, I think, would deny that there was a man called Jesus who lived in Judaea in the first decades of the first century AD. His existence is recorded by the writers of the four

Gospels and also by several distinguished non-Christian historians, including the Roman Tacitus, and the Jew Josephus. We also know beyond doubt how rapidly the Christian faith grew throughout the Roman Empire in the period following the death of Jesus. Well before the end of the first century there was a sufficiently large number of Christians all over the Mediterranean area to provoke a hostile reaction from the authorities, culminating in several waves of vicious persecution in which large numbers of Christians – probably tens of thousands – were killed.

Quite simply, this means that within the lifetime of those who were eyewitnesses of the crucial events a religion was born and spread rapidly, a religion which claimed that its founder, executed by the Roman authorities, had risen from the dead. No amount of argument over detail about the crucifixion and burial of Jesus can obscure this. Both the believers and their opponents recognised it. The latter were desperate to disprove the Christian case but were demonstrably unable to do so. Unlike us today, they had access to the eyewitnesses. They could cross-examine them and search for flaws or discrepancies in their story. Surely it shouldn't have been impossible, given the ingenuity and resources of the Empire, to demolish so incredible an argument as that a man had risen from the dead? The will certainly existed, but the evidence of history is that they utterly failed to do so.

An Age of Cynicism

Modern people will say that those were gullible days, when superstitious people were prepared to believe in almost anything. In fact, that is not the case. The first century was an age of cynicism and rationalism. The dominant school of Greek thought was Stoicism and one of the two major Jewish groups were the Sadducees. Both adamantly rejected any idea of life after death. Even the disciples of Jesus, who had seen his miracles, still jibbed at belief in his resurrection – just look at the story of the disciple Thomas (John 20:24–9)!

So, from two assertions that are very nearly undeniable we are able to argue the strength of the case for the resurrection. These assertions are:

- Jesus really existed;
- Soon after his death a major religion grew rapidly throughout the Roman Empire, claiming that he had risen from the dead.

Those who reject the resurrection must find a more credible explanation for these twin facts. Frankly, nobody has yet done so. Professor C.F.D. Moule asks a sharp question: 'If the coming into existence [of the Christian Church] rips

> " *History teaches us that people will suffer for their convictions but not for their inventions. We tell lies to get out of trouble, not to get into it. The whip and the sword soon uncover fraud.* "
>
> (John Young)

a great hole in history, a hole the size and shape of Resurrection, what does the secular historian propose to stop it up with?'

Of course, the case for the resurrection of Jesus goes further than that. On the third day after his death, his disciples found his tomb to be empty. That is an important

piece of evidence, because the burial of an executed public figure like Jesus is not a hole-in-the-corner affair. But when the disciples found the tomb empty, and said so publicly, the authorities were unable to counter their story. They did not produce the body of Jesus. They did not explain the folded grave-clothes or the rolling back of the massive stone. The only explanation found in contemporary records was the rather pathetic one that this and all the miracles of Jesus were demonic in origin.

However, it goes further than simply an empty tomb. The disciples claimed to have seen Jesus alive, active and vocal. According to the apostle Paul, writing a mere twenty years or so after the event, 'more than five hundred brethren' saw him on one occasion (1 Corinthians 15:6). Not only that, but, he adds, 'most of whom are still alive'. That is the claim of a confident man. 'Look', he says, in effect, 'if you don't believe me, find them, and interview them yourself.' Here Paul is presenting Christianity as it ought always to be presented, as an historical religion, rooted in certain events that actually happened at a place in geography and a date in history. It is certainly much more than a matter of wishful thinking. The Christian belief that Jesus rose from the dead, and the evidence for it, are for many people the conclusive evidence that death is not necessarily the end of human life.

Section 2 *What kind of 'body'?*

I've said that Christians don't think of life after death in terms of spirits and ghostly bodies, but in that case, how do they think of the human body after death? That question is highly relevant to any discussion of life beyond the grave, because one of the biggest difficulties people have with the idea is that they can't begin to imagine what we, or our loved ones, would be like taken out of this space-time world which we inhabit.

The only helpful answer I know is the case of the only person who has come back from the grave to show us, and that, once again, is Jesus. His resurrection, and the nature of his risen body, are the strongest clues we have as to what life beyond death might be like.

Take, for instance, the apparently simple question: 'What was it those Christian eyewitnesses of the risen Jesus actually saw?' It isn't enough to say that they 'saw' or 'met' Jesus. In what form did they see or meet him? Was he in every way exactly the same as he had been before his death? And if not, what had changed?

When we start to consider those questions, two contrasting impressions may well come into our minds. The first – almost undeniable, from the Gospel evidence – is that the appearance of Jesus was changed, and changed to such an extent or in such a way that even his closest friends failed to recognise him at first. On the morning of the resurrection Mary Magdalene supposed he was 'the gardener' (John 20:15). Two of the disciples walked seven miles to Emmaus with him on the same day and did not recognise him until a familiar mannerism connected with giving thanks for the evening meal 'opened their eyes' (Luke 24:30, 31). Peter and the other disciples needed, and were given, other evidence than that of their eyes that the stranger who had prepared breakfast for them on the shore of Galilee was in fact Jesus (John 21:1–13).

However, it was not only his appearance that seems to have been changed. Although the risen Jesus specifically denied that he was a ghost or spirit (Luke 24:38, 39), and although he had 'flesh and bones' as the disciples could see (Luke 24:39–43), yet he was able to enter rooms through locked doors (John 20:19), appear in places many miles apart without travelling by any conventional means, and was eventually 'taken from their sight' on the mount of the Ascension (Acts 1:9). It's hardly necessary to say that none of these things is feasible for a human body and in fact none of these things happened to Jesus during his earthly life. Before his resurrection Jesus' body was unquestionably that of a normal human being. He got tired and hungry. He needed rest and sleep. If he had to travel it was on foot or ass's back. And when they nailed him to a cross, he died. We can understand that. It's what being a normal man or woman is like.

Not Mortal but Immortal

Yet after the resurrection all this was changed. The body he now had was not mortal but immortal. As St Paul puts it, 'Christ being raised from the dead will never die again' (Romans 6:9). The new body of Jesus was not subject to the onslaught of disease, accident or growing old.

In fact, and put simply, this was not an 'earthly' body at all. It was undoubtedly real. The witnesses were not wrong about that. They saw and met Jesus as a complete human being – body, mind and spirit, as we say. But it was not an earth-bound body. In the time between his death and resurrection, it had undergone a fundamental change.

So it is undeniable that the body of Jesus had changed at his resurrection. But it is also undeniable, if we assume that the

> "A belief in immortality has therapeutic power, because no one can live in peace in a house that he knows is shortly to tumble about his ears. "
>
> (Karl Jung)

witnesses are at all reliable, that Jesus before and after the resurrection was the same person. No matter what extraordinary changes had taken place in his bodily properties or form, all who knew him well had no doubt at all who he was. They 'knew' it was the Lord (John 21:12). They recognised him not so much by what he looked like but by what he was. This was the man they had known and loved so well – no doubt about it. Mary Magdalene recognised his voice. The disciples at Emmaus recognised his manner. The disciples by the lake recognised his characteristic action. In other words, they recognised the person, and were prepared to die for that belief.

This evidence about the resurrection of Jesus is important for what it tells us about the whole matter of life beyond death. The Bible tells us that what happened to Jesus will one day happen to all those who trust in him – he is the 'prototype' of all our 'resurrections'. In the ringing words of St Paul: 'The trumpet will sound, and the dead will be raised imperishable, and we shall be changed, in the twinkling of an eye' (1 Corinthians 15:52). These bodies are mortal, and they die. They are made for earth and in the end they return to the earth. It is not part of Christian faith to believe that the flesh and blood and bones in which we live now have any future beyond this life. What I need is a new body in which my 'spirit' – the real 'me' – can go on expressing myself.

> "*All shall be Amen and Alleluia.*
>
> *We shall rest and we shall see.*
> *We shall see and we shall know.*
> *We shall know and we shall love.*
> *We shall love and we shall praise.*
> *Behold our end, which is no end.*" (St Augustine of Hippo)

One scientist (Sir John Houghton, in his book *The Search for God – Can Science Help?*) draws an interesting analogy. If we compare the human body to the hardware of a computer, and the 'self' or spirit to the software, at death we can think of the hardware failing and being disposed of, but the software becoming available for use in new hardware, a new 'body' which will be more advanced, capable of previously undreamt of possibilities. Many of us have seen software from a failed, old computer being transformed in a spanking new version. It's quite a thought that something similar might happen to us after death!

Oddly enough, it's uncannily similar to an image offered by St Paul in discussing the relationship between the human body that dies and the resurrection body that it becomes. He wasn't into computers, of course, but drew a similar analogy from the world of horticulture. The question he was answering was, 'How are the dead raised? With what kind of body do they come?' and his answer was to compare the seed which is sown in the ground (which eventually dies and ceases to exist) with the plant which grows from it. The plant may not look remotely like the seed, but it has a continuity of life with it and certainly develops from it. St Paul goes on to make the point that what is 'sown' when a human being dies is physical, but that what is raised is spiritual: 'Flesh and blood cannot inherit the kingdom of heaven' (1 Corinthians 15:35–50).

That fits in perfectly with what we saw about the resurrection of Jesus. He was the 'same person' – the witnesses were very clear about that. But he was 'changed'. That change was from physical to spiritual, from a body suited to life in first-century Palestine to a body suited to life in heaven with God for ever. What St Paul confirms is wonderful beyond words: what was true of Jesus will be true of us, and of those we love. In every respect that really matters, in all that we truly are, we shall not die. All we shall do is move from one mode of self-expression to another, from one kind of life – earthly life – to another – eternal life: from what is fading away to what lives for ever. That sounds like good news to me.

Section 3 *What is heaven like?*

A good deal of the scepticism about life after death seems to centre on the ideas people have about heaven. I must admit that some of the old hymns and spirituals, and folk memories, too, evoke images that are enough to make any normal person want to be somewhere else. 'Gathering by the river' doesn't especially appeal to me, nor does the notion of angels harping away for all eternity. Nor even, to be honest, does the image presented by the Victorian hymn: 'Prostrate before thy throne to lie, and gaze and gaze on Thee'. All right for a century or two, I suppose, but tending to the tedious if it went on for much longer than that!

> *"Man is the only animal that contemplates death, and also the only animal that shows any doubt of its finality. ""*
> (William Ernest Hocking)

However, these are no more than pictures, based partly on a literal reading of Scripture and partly on the imagination of the hymn-writer. For an age in which poverty and epidemic made death a domestic commonplace they were probably helpful and comforting. In any case, the truth is that the Bible offers us nothing more concrete than pictures and analogies of heaven. It is up to us to interpret them.

Jesus spoke a lot about 'the kingdom of heaven'. Indeed, he constantly said: 'The kingdom of heaven is like ...' – and then went on to offer us more pictures: a field with both corn and weeds in it; a net, enclosing a vast catch; a tree, growing from a tiny seed; treasure hidden in a field; and a pearl of great value. All of these images speak of life and growth, of beauty and value, of challenge and opportunity. That, said Jesus, is what heaven is 'like'.

He said nothing about how extensive it is, or where it is located, or what it looks like, but he made it clear that God his Father is there – indeed, heaven is where he is. And he also said that it has many 'dwelling-places' (John 14:2)

– 'mansions' in the King James Version's rather exotic translation – and that he would prepare some of them for his disciples. This is not the language of literal facts, of course. Indeed, it is nearer the language of poetry. We can read the words, but we have to use imagination to grasp something of their meaning.

Visions of Heaven

This is even more so when we turn to the visions described in the book of Revelation, the last book of the Bible. Here, John, apparently in some kind of spiritual trance (1:10), saw a series of intense visions of the world beyond this one. They include several beautiful pictures of heaven, which have become part of the scenery for most Christians when they think about the future. Of course, they are visions, not literal descriptions. This distinction would not have caused problems for his contemporaries (who were familiar with this kind of writing) but seems to pose enormous difficulties for modern people.

At the heart of all of these visions of heaven are three elements:

- Heaven is where God and Christ are. Indeed, they are the centre of it, the whole of its life revolving around 'the throne of God';
- People are there, vast numbers of them – 'a multitude that no one could count' – from every nation, tribe, people and language (7:9);

- It involves the total abolition of all that is evil. This is a place without anger, hatred, lying, suffering, pain or death. In vivid imagery we are shown the victory of God over all that is evil.

And that's it, really. All the beautiful pictures of golden streets, harvests twelve times a year, jewel-encrusted gates and trees with healing leaves are there to say that this is a perfect place to be. The city's gates aren't locked because there aren't any thieves. Heaven is all we could wish for, all that human life struggles and longs for.

> " *We should be envisaging a freedom from the confinement of time and space which will make it possible for us to be with all our friends at once and individually, to be enjoying an infinite variety of things as we choose, without delay or hurry, crowding or isolation. It is something new, a new quality of life.* "
>
> (Gillian Evans)

So the Bible's answer to the question 'What is heaven like?' is – well, use your imagination! This is a place of fulfilment, of growth, discovery and endless activity – 'his servants will serve him'. It is a place where we shall be more alive than we have ever been, more loving and more loved. It is, in a memorable phrase of the apostle Paul's, the place where 'together we will be with the Lord for ever' (1 Thessalonians 4:17) – and the 'together' refers to those who have died before us (4:13). No wonder he adds, 'Encourage one another with these words.'

Section 4 *Who goes to heaven?*

The other question that bothers people about life after death is perhaps the most difficult of all: who will be there? For much of Christian history human beings have trembled at the thought of the dreadful Day of Judgement that lies ahead. On that day, the 'good' will be welcomed into heaven and the 'evil' consigned to the fires of hell. In more recent times, preachers have tended to keep quiet on the subject, the fear of hell being used as an incentive to faith even less frequently than the promise of heaven.

However, it still worries people. In popular folk religion, just about everybody goes to heaven, even if by the skin of their teeth, mainly because, well, we'd let them in, wouldn't we, and surely God is kinder than we are? Hell, if it exists at all, is reserved for popular hate figures – Adolf Hitler, Osama bin Laden and perhaps child molesters and murderers. As a vicar, I was asked by anxious partners, 'Will my husband be in heaven? He wasn't very religious, I'm afraid.' I have even had it put to me that if the loved one wasn't going to be in heaven, then they didn't want to go there either.

To all such questions, there is simply no convincing answer, and perhaps God intends it that way. There is actually very little about 'hell' in the New Testament, and what there is comes, rather surprisingly, from the lips of

> *"All we know of what they do above,
> Is that they happy are, and that they love."*
>
> (Edmund Waller)

Jesus. But for him it was Gehenna, the place where the city rubbish was destroyed by fire. 'Hell', in other words, was where the world's rubbish and filth would be finally disposed of. Without it, heaven wouldn't be heaven at all.

A Merciful Judge

What we do know from the Bible is that the world will be judged by the world's Saviour, Jesus Christ. St Paul speaks of the time when, 'according to my gospel', 'God, through Jesus Christ, will judge the secret thoughts of all' (Romans 2:16). That offers a wonderful paradox of the judgement and mercy of God – the world will be judged, even its secret thoughts, but by the very One he sent to die for our sins! The same paradox is embodied in a striking image in the book of Revelation, where seated on the judgement throne at the centre of everything are God and . . . 'the Lamb'. Not only that, but this Lamb 'has the marks of slaughter upon him' (Revelation 5:6, 7:9). The Lamb is, of course, Jesus (John 1:36) and the marks of slaughter are the marks of his crucifixion, when he died 'for the sins of the world'. He is its Saviour, and he is to be its judge.

Nothing could speak more eloquently of God's love for his fallen and fallible children than that. Whatever happens beyond death, I am convinced that no one will be able to shake a fist at God and say, 'You weren't fair!' As the Old Testament declares, 'Shall not the Judge of all the earth do right?' (Genesis 18:25).

That, however, would be too negative a note on which to end. 'God is love', St John declares boldly (1 John 4:16). Love is his very nature. In that love he not only made us for earth, but also held out the wonderful prospect of eternal life with him in heaven. It was in pursuit of that purpose that he sent Jesus into the world, to call people to turn from their old lives and embrace a new way of living. Through his death our past sins and failures can be forgiven. Through his resurrection, we can follow him into the place his Father has prepared for us.

There is a lot more living to be done, in unimaginable realms of the spirit. 'You believe in God,' Jesus said. 'Believe also in me'. Through that faith – even if it's as tiny as a seed of mustard – we can all share the wonder of what lies beyond the barrier which mortals call death.

> *"I pray... that we may merrily meet in heaven"*
>
> (Sir Thomas More, in a letter to his daughter, as he awaited execution under Henry VIII)